WHO A... Football

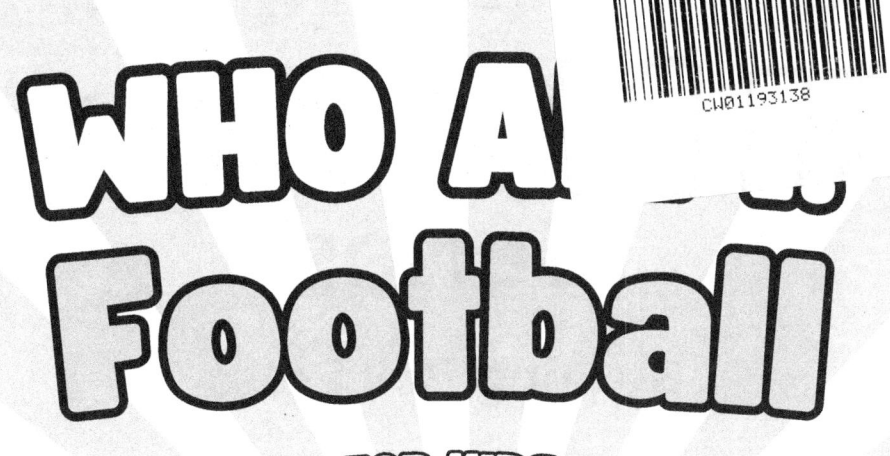

FOR KIDS

CAN YOU GUESS THE PLAYER?

WHO?

100 PLAYERS TO GUESS

The 'Who Am I?' Series

By Long Ball Press

Long Ball Press are an independent publishing team that aims to produce the best activity books possible for our readers.

If you enjoyed using the book as much as we enjoyed making it, then we would love you to leave a review on Amazon so we can hear all about it.

These books are designed to educate young children in a thought-provoking and engaging manner, and we hope you have fun!!

ISBN: 9798863259642

Copyright © 2023 by Long Ball Press

All rights reserved.

No portion of this book may be reproduced in any form without written permission from the publisher or author.

Welcome to Football Who am I!

How To Play:

In this book, there are 100 past and present football players that you need to guess. For each player, there are three clues to help you figure out who it is.

Here's an example:

Clue 1:
I've played for Real Madrid and Bayern Munich.

Clue 2:
I can play left-back and centre-back.

Clue 3:
I have played more than 100 games for Austria.

I am:

David Alaba

We've given you the answer for this one, but you won't be so lucky for the remaining 100!!

Good Luck!!

Who Am I?

Clue 1:
I'm a retired Spanish goalkeeper.

Clue 2:
I won the World Cup in 2010 as captain.

Clue 3:
I spent most of my club career at Real Madrid.

I am:

_____

Who Am I?

Clue 1:
I'm retired, but I played in midfield for England.

Clue 2:
I won the Champions League in 2005.

Clue 3:
I used to score screamers from outside the box.

I am:

_____

Who Am I?

Clue 1:
I won the U17 World Cup in 2017 with England.

Clue 2:
I usually have a very simple haircut.

Clue 3:
I won the treble with Man City in 2023.

I am:

_____

Who Am I?

Clue 1:
I won the World Cup with France in 2018.

Clue 2:
I have played for Juventus and Man United.

Clue 3:
I'm often known for my crazy dancing.

I am:

_____

Who Am I?

Clue 1:
I'm well known for my amazing speed.

Clue 2:
I have scored a hat-trick in a World Cup final.

Clue 3:
I have played with Messi and Neymar.

I am:

_____

Who Am I?

Clue 1:
I am known as the 'Portuguese Magnifico'.

Clue 2:
I have played for Udinese and Sporting Lisbon.

Clue 3:
I have captained Manchester United.

I am:

_____

Who Am I?

Clue 1:
I moved to Barcelona from Ajax in 2019.

Clue 2:
I play in midfield and I'm amazing at passing.

Clue 3:
I play for The Netherlands internationally.

I am:

_____

Who Am I?

Clue 1:
I've won the Ballon d'Or more than anyone else.

Clue 2:
I'm often compared to Maradona.

Clue 3:
I won the World Cup in 2022 in Qatar.

I am:

_____

Who Am I?

Clue 1:
I have a smiley face tattooed behind my ear.

Clue 2:
I'm a goalkeeper who's great at passing.

Clue 3:
I'm Brazilian and I've won the Premier League.

I am:

_____

Who Am I?

Clue 1:
I'm a retired Brazilian footballer.

Clue 2:
I was very successful at Barcelona.

Clue 3:
I've won the World Cup and the Ballon d'Or.

I am:

_____

Who Am I?

Clue 1:
I won the Premier League more than five times.

Clue 2:
I played in midfield for Man United.

Clue 3:
I was well known for my ginger hair.

I am:

_____

Who Am I?

Clue 1:
I won the Ballon d'Or award in 2018.

Clue 2:
I've won multiple Champions League titles.

Clue 3:
I used to play for Tottenham before Real Madrid.

I am:

_____

Who Am I?

Clue 1:
I scored the winning goal in the 2010 World Cup.

Clue 2:
I'm known for my amazing passing and dribbling.

Clue 3:
I spent most of my career at Barcelona.

I am:

_____

Who Am I?

Clue 1:
I'm Real Madrid's all-time top goalscorer.

Clue 2:
I moved to the Saudi Pro League in 2023.

Clue 3:
I have won multiple Ballon d'Or awards.

I am:

_____

Who Am I?

Clue 1:
I am Tottenham's all-time top goalscorer.

Clue 2:
I once played for Leicester City on loan.

Clue 3:
I missed a penalty for England in the 2022 World Cup.

I am:

_____

Who Am I?

Clue 1:
I have played over 100 games for Man United.

Clue 2:
I've done a lot of charity work for young children.

Clue 3:
I'm fast and I made my Man United debut in 2016.

I am:

_____

Who Am I?

Clue 1:
I have played for Borussia Dortmund.

Clue 2:
I won the treble with Man City in 2023.

Clue 3:
I'm tall, strong and I score lots of goals.

I am:

_____

Who Am I?

Clue 1:
I'm a retired right-back that played for Brazil.

Clue 2:
I won more than 40 trophies during my career.

Clue 3:
I have played for Barcelona and PSG.

I am:

_____

Who Am I?

Clue 1:
I moved to Chelsea for £50m in 2011.

Clue 2:
I used to wear a headband when I played.

Clue 3:
I scored in the final of Euro 2008.

I am:

_____

Who Am I?

Clue 1:
I was known by many as 'The White Pele'.

Clue 2:
I am Man United's all-time top goalscorer.

Clue 3:
I had my own TV show called 'Street Striker'.

I am:

_____

Who Am I?

Clue 1:
I am the World Cup's all-time top goalscorer.

Clue 2:
I won the World Cup in 2014 with Germany.

Clue 3:
I'm also Germany's all-time top scorer.

I am:

_____

Who Am I?

Clue 1:
I moved to Man City from Valencia in 2010.

Clue 2:
I won the Premier League with Man City in 2012.

Clue 3:
One of my nicknames is 'El Mago'.

I am:

_____

Who Am I?

Clue 1:
I spent my youth career at Birmingham City.

Clue 2:
I have captained Borussia Dortmund.

Clue 3:
I moved to Real Madrid in the summer of 2023.

I am:

_____

Who Am I?

Clue 1:
I am known as the 'Egyptian King' by many fans.

Clue 2:
I have played for FC Basel and Chelsea.

Clue 3:
I am a right-winger with a deadly left foot.

I am:

_____

Who Am I?

Clue 1:
I'm a Brazilian winger and I'm very fast.

Clue 2:
I scored in the 2022 Champions League final.

Clue 3:
I signed for Real Madrid from Flamengo.

I am:

_____

Who Am I?

Clue 1:
I played in the Man City youth academy.

Clue 2:
I missed a penalty in the Euro 2020 final.

Clue 3:
I moved to Borussia Dortmund in 2017.

I am:

_____

Who Am I?

Clue 1:
I made my debut for Arsenal as a left-back.

Clue 2:
I also missed a penalty in the Euro 2020 final.

Clue 3:
I now play as a right-winger and I'm left-footed.

I am:

_____

Who Am I?

Clue 1:
I have played for Liverpool, Man City and Chelsea.

Clue 2:
I'm English, but I was born in Jamaica.

Clue 3:
I scored more than 90 goals for Man City.

I am:

_____

Who Am I?

Clue 1:
I have played for Bayern Munich and Barcelona.

Clue 2:
I scored the opening goal of Euro 2012.

Clue 3:
I am Polish and I've scored over 300 career goals.

I am:

_____

Who Am I?

Clue 1:
I won the Champions League in 2020.

Clue 2:
I play international football for Canada.

Clue 3:
I play as a left-back and I'm known for my speed.

I am:

_____

Who Am I?

Clue 1:
I played for Lyon before moving to Real Madrid.

Clue 2:
I won the Ballon d'Or award in 2022.

Clue 3:
I have won the Champions League five times.

I am:

_____

Who Am I?

Clue 1:
I have played for Man City and Chelsea.

Clue 2:
I was part of Belgium's 'golden generation'.

Clue 3:
I have been injured in a Champions League final twice.

I am:

_____

Who Am I?

Clue 1:
I scored 147 goals for Chelsea from midfield.

Clue 2:
I have been Everton and Chelsea manager.

Clue 3:
I have exactly the same name as my dad.

I am:

_____

Who Am I?

Clue 1:
I won the treble with Man United in 1999.

Clue 2:
I was sent off in the 1998 World Cup.

Clue 3:
I famously moved to LA Galaxy in 2007.

I am:

_____

Who Am I?

Clue 1:
I played for Santos before moving to Europe.

Clue 2:
I have broken the transfer fee record.

Clue 3:
I'm Brazilian and I'm known for my skills and flair.

I am:

_____

Who Am I?

Clue 1:
I have won the Champions league four times.

Clue 2:
I spent most of my career playing for Barcelona.

Clue 3:
I'm a Spanish centre back who's played in England.

I am:
_____

Who Am I?

Clue 1:
I scored a penalty in the Euro 2020 final.

Clue 2:
I have captained Manchester United.

Clue 3:
I have also played for Leicester City.

I am:

_____

Who Am I?

Clue 1:
I have scored in a Champions League final.

Clue 2:
I have played for Tottenham and Real Madrid.

Clue 3:
Outside of football, I enjoy playing golf.

I am:

_____

Who Am I?

Clue 1:
I'm a defender, but I've scored many penalties.

Clue 2:
I signed for PSG in the same summer as Messi.

Clue 3:
I have won many Champions League titles.

I am:

_____

Who Am I?

Clue 1:
I signed for Chelsea in the summer of 2012.

Clue 2:
I was part of Belgium's 'golden generation'.

Clue 3:
I won the Champions League in 2022.

I am:

_____

Who Am I?

Clue 1:
I scored a penalty in the 2022 World Cup Final.

Clue 2:
I have played for Roma and Juventus.

Clue 3:
I have a famous mask celebration when I score.

I am:

_____

Who Am I?

Clue 1:
I was sent off in the 2006 World Cup Final.

Clue 2:
I'm retired, but I used to play in midfield.

Clue 3:
I'm French and I've managed Real Madrid.

I am:

_____

Who Am I?

Clue 1:
I have played for Southampton and Liverpool.

Clue 2:
I'm a fast Senegalese Winger.

Clue 3:
I scored the fastest Premier League hat-trick ever.

I am:

_____

Who Am I?

Clue 1:
I was once sent off for biting another player.

Clue 2:
I have played alongside Messi and Neymar.

Clue 3:
I won the Champions League in 2015.

I am:

_____

Who Am I?

Clue 1:
I've played for Brazil at senior, U20 and U23 level.

Clue 2:
I moved to Man City in January 2017.

Clue 3:
I used to play for Palmeiras before Man City.

I am:

_____

Who Am I?

Clue 1:
I spent 15 years at Real Madrid from 2007-2022.

Clue 2:
I'm one of the best left-backs ever.

Clue 3:
I'm best friends with Cristiano Ronaldo.

I am:

_____

Who Am I?

Clue 1:
I'm well known for my 'take the L' dance.

Clue 2:
I've spent most of my career in Spain.

Clue 3:
I won the 2018 World Cup with France.

I am:

_____

Who Am I?

Clue 1:
I have two dogs called Atom and Humber.

Clue 2:
I have played in France, England, Spain and Italy.

Clue 3:
I am considered the best Chilean player ever.

I am:

_____

Who Am I?

Clue 1:
I have played for Bayern Munich and Real Madrid.

Clue 2:
I'm a midfielder and I'm known for my great passing.

Clue 3:
I was part of the Germany team that beat Brazil 7-1.

I am:

_____

Who Am I?

Clue 1:
I moved to Man United from PSV in 2015.

Clue 2:
I've played more than 80 times for The Netherlands.

Clue 3:
I have also played for Barcelona and Atletico Madrid.

I am:

_____

Who Am I?

Clue 1:
I'm considered to be one of the best goalkeepers ever.

Clue 2:
I moved from Schalke to Bayern Munich in 2011.

Clue 3:
I was one of the first-ever 'sweeper keepers'.

I am:

_____

Who Am I?

Clue 1:
I scored in the 2021 Champions League final.

Clue 2:
I played in the Bayer Leverkusen academy.

Clue 3:
I moved to Arsenal in the summer of 2023.

I am:

_____

Who Am I?

Clue 1:
I started my career at R.S.C Anderlecht.

Clue 2:
I am well known for my strength and power.

Clue 3:
I've played for both Chelsea and Inter.

I am:

_____

Who Am I?

Clue 1:
I once scored an amazing scorpion kick.

Clue 2:
I'm France's all-time top goalscorer.

Clue 3:
I won Ligue 1 with Montpellier in 2012.

I am:

_____

Who Am I?

Clue 1:
I played for Argentina in the 2022 World Cup.

Clue 2:
I signed for Inter from Racing Club in 2018.

Clue 3:
I used to be a defender when I was young.

I am:

_____

Who Am I?

Clue 1:
I scored in the 2011 Champions League final.

Clue 2:
I have played for Barcelona and Chelsea.

Clue 3:
I've played more than 60 games for Spain.

I am:

_____

Who Am I?

Clue 1:
I was once the most expensive defender ever.

Clue 2:
I have captained the Brazilian national team.

Clue 3:
I played over 200 games for Paris Saint-Germain.

I am:

_____

Who Am I?

Clue 1:
I moved to Man City from Monaco in 2017.

Clue 2:
I am 5ft 8in but I'm a very technical player.

Clue 3:
I'm Portuguese and I've also played for Benfica.

I am:

_____

Who Am I?

Clue 1:
I look like a bodybuilder and I'm very fast.

Clue 2:
I played more than 150 games for Wolves.

Clue 3:
I have also played for Barcelona during my career.

I am:

_____

Who Am I?

Clue 1:
I was the captain of France in the 2018 World Cup.

Clue 2:
I joined Tottenham in the summer of 2012.

Clue 3:
I'm one of the best goalkeepers of all-time.

I am:

_____

Who Am I?

Clue 1:
I'm a 6ft 7in goalkeeper from Belgium.

Clue 2:
I won the Champions League in 2022.

Clue 3:
I have played for 2 Spanish rivals in my career.

I am:

_____

Who Am I?

Clue 1:
I have played for Man United and Watford.

Clue 2:
I'm a former goalkeeper who retired in 2023.

Clue 3:
I have a very successful YouTube channel.

I am:

_____

Who Am I?

Clue 1:
My nickname in football is 'El Matador'.

Clue 2:
I am Uruguay's 2nd top goalscorer ever.

Clue 3:
I have long black hair and wear a headband.

I am:

_____

Who Am I?

Clue 1:
I missed a penalty in the Euro 2020 final.

Clue 2:
I moved to Chelsea from Napoli in 2018.

Clue 3:
I have a unique style of taking penalties.

I am:

_____

Who Am I?

Clue 1:
I won the 'Golden Boy' award in 2016.

Clue 2:
I have played for Bayern Munich and Swansea.

Clue 3:
I made my debut for Portugal in 2016.

I am:

_____

Who Am I?

Clue 1:
I have to play football with a pacemaker.

Clue 2:
I have played over 120 times for Denmark.

Clue 3:
I spent seven years at Tottenham Hotspur.

I am:

_____

Who Am I?

Clue 1:
I won the Premier League with Leicester.

Clue 2:
I'm well known for being a great dribbler.

Clue 3:
I moved to the Saudi Pro League in 2023.

I am:

_____

Who Am I?

Clue 1:
I'm one of the best defensive midfielders ever.

Clue 2:
I spent almost all of my career at Barcelona.

Clue 3:
I made my Barcelona debut in 2008.

I am:

_____

Who Am I?

Clue 1:
I wore the shirt number 26 during my career.

Clue 2:
I'm retired, but used to be a centre-back.

Clue 3:
I won my first Premier League title in 2005.

I am:

_____

Who Am I?

Clue 1:
I signed for Man City from Atletico Madrid.

Clue 2:
I'm retired, but I used to be a striker.

Clue 3:
I'm Argentinian and best friends with Lionel Messi

I am:

_____

Who Am I?

Clue 1:
I've played for Leeds, West Ham and Man United.

Clue 2:
I'm regarded as one of the best defenders ever.

Clue 3:
I won the Champions League in 2008.

I am:

_____

Who Am I?

Clue 1:
I used to play as a defender for Liverpool.

Clue 2:
I missed a penalty in the 2006 World Cup for England.

Clue 3:
I now work as a presenter on Sky Sports.

I am:

_____

Who Am I?

Clue 1:
I won the Premier League with Leicester.

Clue 2:
I love to celebrate in front of opposition fans.

Clue 3:
I drink a red bull before every single match.

I am:

_____

Who Am I?

Clue 1:
I made my Arsenal debut at 16 years old.

Clue 2:
I won the Premier League, but not with Arsenal.

Clue 3:
I'm Spanish and I also played for Barcelona.

I am:

_____

Who Am I?

Clue 1:
I played in the Man United youth academy.

Clue 2:
I'm well known for my crazy dance moves.

Clue 3:
In 2022, I moved to Nottingham Forrest.

I am:

_____

Who Am I?

Clue 1:
I played more than 400 games for Man United.

Clue 2:
I moved from Atletico Madrid in 2012.

Clue 3:
I'm a goalkeeper who has amazing reactions.

I am:

_____

Who Am I?

Clue 1:
I was born in Sunderland, but left in 2011.

Clue 2:
I've played in three Champions League finals.

Clue 3:
I was the captain of Liverpool before leaving in 2023.

I am:

_____

Who Am I?

Clue 1:
I was once known as the next 'wonderkid'.

Clue 2:
I played more than 150 games for Tottenham.

Clue 3:
I'm a midfielder and I love the number 20 shirt.

I am:

_____

Who Am I?

Clue 1:
I was Sir Alex Ferguson's last-ever signing.

Clue 2:
I am best known for my time at Crystal Palace.

Clue 3:
I have played for England and Ivory Coast.

I am:

_____

Who Am I?

Clue 1:
I played in Southampton's youth academy.

Clue 2:
I'm a left back and I was badly injured in 2015.

Clue 3:
I have played more than 150 games for Man united.

I am:

_____

Who Am I?

Clue 1:
I have played for both Brazil and Spain.

Clue 2:
I'm a striker and I once played for Chelsea.

Clue 3:
I'm known for my aggression and feisty attitude.

I am:

_____

Who Am I?

Clue 1:
I assisted Sergio Aguero's famous goal in 2012.

Clue 2:
I've played for more than ten teams in my career.

Clue 3:
I'm known for my phrase 'why always me'.

I am:

_____

Who Am I?

Clue 1:
I've been named German player of the year five times.

Clue 2:
I played for Real Madrid between 2010-2013.

Clue 3:
I played more than 180 games for Arsenal.

I am:

_____

Who Am I?

Clue 1:
I won my only Premier League title in 2013.

Clue 2:
I played for both Arsenal and Man United.

Clue 3:
I'm retired, but I used to be a striker.

I am:

_____

Who Am I?

Clue 1:
I have won the Premier League and the World Cup.

Clue 2:
I'm a midfielder and I'm known for my amazing stamina.

Clue 3:
I'm French and I moved to Al-Ittihad in 2023.

I am:

_____

Who Am I?

Clue 1:
I'm one of the best midfielders of all-time.

Clue 2:
I won the Champions League four times.

Clue 3:
I had a great partnership with Andres Iniesta.

I am:

_____

Who Am I?

Clue 1:
I scored in the 2022 World Cup final.

Clue 2:
I have played for Real Madrid, PSG and Man United.

Clue 3:
My nickname is 'Fideo', Spanish for noodle.

I am:

_____

Who Am I?

Clue 1:
I was once dubbed 'the next Thierry Henry'.

Clue 2:
I signed for Man United in the summer of 2015.

Clue 3:
I scored on my Man United debut vs Liverpool.

I am:

_____

Who Am I?

Clue 1:
I played over 150 games for Liverpool.

Clue 2:
I signed for Barcelona in 2018 for £140m.

Clue 3:
I'm a Brazilian attacking midfielder.

I am:

_____

Who Am I?

Clue 1:
I won the World Cup with Spain in 2010.

Clue 2:
I have played for Valencia, Man United and Chelsea.

Clue 3:
I won the Champions League in 2012.

I am:

_____

Who Am I?

Clue 1:
I'm Dutch, but I spent most of my career in Germany.

Clue 2:
I'm retired, but I was a winger with a great left foot.

Clue 3:
I scored in the 2013 Champions League final.

I am:

_____

Who Am I?

Clue 1:
David Moyes was my manager twice in my career.

Clue 2:
I have played in multiple World Cups for Belgium.

Clue 3:
I am well known for my giant frizzy hair.

I am:

_____

Who Am I?

Clue 1:
I scored in the 2014 World Cup final for Germany.

Clue 2:
I've spent a lot of my senior career injured.

Clue 3:
I've played over 150 games for Borussia Dortmund.

I am:

_____

Who Am I?

Clue 1:
I once scored an amazing free kick vs Crystal Palace.

Clue 2:
I'm French and I was a fan favourite at West Ham.

Clue 3:
I have played for Marseille twice in my career.

I am:

_____

Who Am I?

Clue 1:
I'm retired, but I played over 100 games for Portugal.

Clue 2:
I used to do a backflip when I scored.

Clue 3:
I was a winger and I played for Man United.

I am:

_____

Who Am I?

Clue 1:
I won five Champions Leagues with Real Madrid

Clue 2:
I'm one of the best defensive midfielders ever.

Clue 3:
I played in the Sao Paulo youth academy.

I am:

_____

Who Am I?

Clue 1:
I'm a Uruguayan striker with long, black hair.

Clue 2:
I moved to Liverpool in the summer of 2022.

Clue 3:
I scored 32 goals in 57 games for Benfica.

I am:

_____

Who Am I?

Clue 1:
I've played for Celtic, Southampton and Liverpool.

Clue 2:
I am a 6ft 5in tall Dutch central defender.

Clue 3:
I have long hair, but I wear it in a ponytail.

I am:

_____

Who Am I?

Clue 1:
I signed for Man City for over £100m in 2021.

Clue 2:
I played more than 180 games for Aston Villa.

Clue 3:
I love to party and celebrate when my team wins.

I am:

_____

Who Am I?

Clue 1:
I've played for both Ireland and England at senior level.

Clue 2:
I have played at centre-back and defensive midfield.

Clue 3:
I captained West Ham for more than three years.

I am:

_____

ANSWER PAGES

Who Am I?

Answers

1. Iker Casillas
2. Steven Gerrard
3. Phil Foden
4. Paul Pogba
5. Kylian Mbappe
6. Bruno Fernandes
7. Frenkie De Jong
8. Lionel Messi
9. Ederson
10. Ronaldinho
11. Paul Scholes
12. Luka Modric
13. Andres Iniesta
14. Cristiano Ronaldo
15. Harry Kane
16. Marcus Rashford
17. Erling Haaland
18. Dani Alves
19. Fernando Torres
20. Wayne Rooney
21. Miroslav Klose
22. David Silva
23. Jude Bellingham
24. Mo Salah
25. Vinicius Junior
26. Jadon Sancho
27. Bukayo Saka
28. Raheem Sterling
29. Robert Lewandowski
30. Alphonso Davies
31. Karim Benzema
32. Kevin De Bruyne
33. Frank Lampard
34. David Beckham
35. Neymar
36. Gerard Pique
37. Harry Maguire
38. Gareth Bale
39. Sergio Ramos
40. Eden Hazard

Who Am I?

Answers

41. Paulo Dybala
42. Zinedine Zidane
43. Sadio Mane
44. Luis Suarez
45. Gabriel Jesus
46. Marcelo
47. Antoine Griezmann
48. Alexis Sanchez
49. Toni Kroos
50. Memphis Depay
51. Manuel Neuer
52. Kai Havertz
53. Romelu Lukaku
54. Olivier Giroud
55. Lautaro Martinez
56. Pedro
57. Thiago Silva
58. Bernardo Silva
59. Adama Traore
60. Hugo Lloris
61. Thibaut Courtois
62. Ben Foster
63. Edinson Cavani
64. Jorginho
65. Renato Sanches
66. Christian Eriksen
67. Riyad Mahrez
68. Sergio Busquets
69. John Terry
70. Sergio Aguero
71. Rio Ferdinand
72. Jamie Carragher
73. Jamie Vardy
74. Cesc Fabregas
75. Jesse Lingard
76. David De Gea
77. Jordan Henderson
78. Dele Alli
79. Wilfred Zaha
80. Luke Shaw

Who Am I?

Answers

81. Diego Costa
82. Mario Balotelli
83. Mesut Ozil
84. Robin van Persie
85. N'Golo Kante
86. Xavi
87. Angel Di Maria.
88. Anthony Martial
89. Philippe Coutinho
90. Juan Mata
91. Arjen Robben
92. Marouane Fellaini
93. Mario Gotze
94. Dimitri Payet
95. Nani
96. Casemiro
97. Darwin Nunez
98. Virgil van Dijk
99. Jack Grealish
100. Declan Rice

Printed in Great Britain
by Amazon